CRYPTS, caves, and tunnels of London

First published in 2002 by Watling St Publishing
The Old Chapel
East End
Northleach
Gloucestershire
GL54 3PQ

Printed in Thailand

Copyright © Watling St Publishing Ltd 2002

ISBN 1-904153-04-6

24681097531

Cover design and illustration: Mark Davis
Cartoons: Martin Angel

CRYPTS, caves, and tunnels of London

Ian Marchant

WATLING STREET

Ian Marchant has written two highly acclaimed novels, *In Southern Waters* and *The Battle for Dole Acre*. He is currently writing a history of the British railways. This is his first book for children.

To Esme and Nelly with love and squalor

Contents

CHAPTER ONE

Buried London

There is an old house in North London whose owner is a historian. He knew that his house was old when he moved in, but he didn't know how old. So he set about finding out. He started by peeling off the top layer of wallpaper in the hall. There was more wallpaper underneath, so he peeled that off too. He kept peeling layer after layer away from the wall, until he reached the original wall covering, a painted pattern which he knew had to come from the 1780s. So he knew that that was when his house had been built.

A city is like that, especially a very old city like London. The city that we see around us today is only the top layer. If we could peel it back we would find the remains of what London has been for over 2000 years, layer after layer, hidden now in the ground. Historians and archaeologists can read the layers, and together they could piece together the story of the cities and towns and villages and fields which are buried under our streets. And if they peeled away enough layers they would come to bare rock: the foundation that London is built on.

Ludd Town rocks

Buried deep underneath it all there is chalk, which in turn is covered by London Clay, brick earth and gravel. There are a series of gravel terraces, running down towards the river, like those on a gravelly beach. The gravel was left there at the end of the last Ice Age, which ended about 13,000 years ago, pushed there by the rivers of ice which flowed as far south as London. This means that London rises slightly the further you go inland from the Thames. Before humans came, London was a great marsh. The Thames was three times wider than it is now, and streams and rivers ran into it. Islands made from the gravel rose slightly higher than the marsh; if you stand outside Westminster Abbey, you are on one of these islands, called Thorney Island. The remains of sharks and crocodiles have been found buried in the clay. Most importantly of all, the river was shallow. This meant that it was the last place before you reached the sea that armies and traders could cross the river, whilst ships could reach the site from the sea.

There had been settlers in the area for thousands of years. Flint axes and Bronze Age weapons have been found all over the London area. If only we could find them, lost under modern London, there are buried houses and settlements going back to the days of the Stone Age. The chief of one of these buried settlements was probably called King Ludd. This long-lost chief gave his name to the huge city we see today.

All that remains of the Romans

It was such a good place to settle that the Roman invaders built their city just here, 2000 years ago. They built it from bricks that they made from the local brick earth. London is still largely built from these bricks, which are called London Stock bricks. So when you look around you, you can really see that London grows from the earth that it is built on. Some of the Roman streets are still there.

Walk down Cheapside, and you are walking down the Romans' high street. The skull of a wolf was found buried here. And if you walk along Aldermanbury, you are following the street which ran alongside the coliseum, where gladiators fought to the death.

The Roman city of Londinium inside its strong walls lasted for over 400 years, until the Roman Empire collapsed, and all the people who lived in the city left it to fall to ruin. For more than 200 years the city stood empty. It was a ghost city. When the Saxon invasions of England started, in about 500 AD, these fierce warriors saw that it was a good place to build a city, just as the Romans had. But they were scared of the old ghost city that lay in ruins, so they built their city alongside it, and called it Lundenwic. That city is buried now, too, under the Strand and Covent Garden. All that remains of the Saxons' city is a place name, the Aldwych, which means the old market.

It was only the arrival of a new tribe of warlike people, the Vikings, in about the year 800, which led the Saxon settlers to move to safety behind the walls of the old ghost city, led by their king, Alfred the Great. Coins have been found buried, which were minted to celebrate Alfred's recapture of the city from Viking invaders. So it was Alfred who started to build on the ruins of the abandoned Roman City. Then, after 1066, the Normans invaded England, and they started to build on top of the old city too. Over hundreds of years, London came back to life, and grew outside its walls, stretching out to meet the King's Palace and the great Abbey which stood on Thorney Island. This became a separate city, called Westminster, and London stretched westward to meet it. In the end, even Thorney Island was buried.

Over hundreds of years more and more people moved to London, looking for work. As well as constantly rebuilding over the old cities, London needed to grow, to the north, south, east and west. Villages like Chelsea and Hampstead were swallowed up, as were towns like Southwark and Islington. In the 20th century, London even covered over a whole county, Middlesex. The Underground Railway extended its lines right up into the country in the 1920s and '30s, and fields and country lanes were swallowed up by suburbs built for the people who took the railway to work in London. If you take the Metropolitan Line out to the far north-west of London, you might try finding the old village of Ruislip, or the tiny hamlet of Eastcote, buried under the neat rows of houses.

The Temple of Audrey

Wherever you are in London, under your feet are the buried remains of the old layers of the city. The people who study these layers are called archaeologists. From the pots and coins and bones and buried treasure that archaeologists find, they can get an idea of what the buried cities were like. But it is not always easy for archaeologists to get permission to dig wherever they like. Usually, they have to wait for others to peel back the layers so that they can get their spades out and discover the buried London. After the Second World War, much of the old City of London had been destroyed by Nazi bombs. The bombs had peeled away many layers, and before people started to rebuild, archaeologists were allowed to investigate.

One of the most important Roman finds in London was discovered during a dig at one of the bomb sites. It is called the Temple of Mithras. Mithras was a sun god, and the most important part of the worship of him was the sacrifice of bulls. The archaeologists didn't know what they would find when they started digging on the old bomb site. Then, in September of 1954, an archaeologist called Audrey Williams made an incredible discovery. She found the head of a statue of Mithras where it had lain in the ground for 1800 years. Over the next few weeks, many more statues of Roman gods were discovered. No one had remembered that the Temple was there for almost 2000 years.

You can see the head of Mithras in the Museum of London, along with many other incredible things that have been found buried in London. The museum is a good place to start if you want to find out more about archaeology in London. London is still adding more layers, building and rebuilding over what was there before. This gives the museum a chance to organize new digs, when old buildings are knocked down, and before new ones are put up. Sometimes you can help on these digs, and there is a Young Archaeologists Club that you can join. Or you could find out what lies buried under your street, by looking at old maps in the library, or by finding out where street names come from.

New finds are being made all the time. In 2000, a fabulous gold and turquoise Celtic brooch was found at a dig in Floral Street, near Covent Garden. You can see that at the Museum of London, too. And who knows? If you started digging, you might find something amazing, like Audrey Williams did. Perhaps even the buried remains of Ludd's Town, or the grave of King Ludd himself. It's there, somewhere, buried beneath the streets, waiting to be found.

Ten cool underground finds.

Flint hand axe - from under the Regent Palace Hotel, Glasshouse Street.

Antler spear - found in the Thames near Wandsworth.

Roman emerald necklace - under Cannon Street.

Iron dagger in its sheath - under Copthall Court, in the City of London.

Glass cremation jar - from the Roman cemetery at Bishopsgate.

Skeleton of a horse - found in Miles Lane.

Gold saxon brooches - found in Hanwell, West London

Viking battle axes - found near London Bridge.

Medieval glass goblet - from Winchester Palace, in Southwark.

The Cheapside Hoard - 230 pieces of jewellery found in Cheapside.

CHAPTER TWO

The Thames Tunnels

There are more than twenty tunnels under the River Thames. Some, like the Blackwall and Rotherhithe Tunnels, carry cars; others, like the new tunnel built for the Jubilee Line Extension, carry trains. Others take water, or electrical cables. There are even two tunnels, at Greenwich and Woolwich, which only take pedestrians. Many thousands of people travel under the Thames every day, most of them without noticing the river running above their heads. But almost 200 years ago, people thought that it was impossible to dig a tunnel under the water.

The madness of Mr Brunel

Then, in 1818, a French engineer named Marc Brunel invented a machine called the tunnelling shield. This machine meant that for the first time, miners could dig in safety, as the shield held up the tunnel roof while they worked. Behind the shield, bricklayers and stonemasons could build an arch which would keep the tunnel safe and dry. Brunel said that his invention meant that it was now possible to dig a tunnel under the Thames and, in 1824, a company was set up to build the world's first underwater tunnel.

Marc Brunel started work by building a great cylinder of bricks above ground at the Rotherhithe end of where the tunnel was to be, 300 feet away from the riverbank. When the cylinder was finished, it was 40 feet high. Then Marc got his workmen (called 'navvies') to dig the ground away from underneath the cylinder so that slowly, inch by inch, it sank into the ground. Now Brunel had built a shaft into the earth, and he was ready to move the shield into place so that they could start to make the tunnel.

The great shield was installed, and the navvies began to dig. All went well at first, and the men could move the shield forward at about a foot a day. But as the tunnel got closer to the actual river, the digging got harder. Instead of the London clay which geologists had said would be there, Brunel found nothing but gravel and silt. The tunnel kept filling with water, and huge steam pumps had to be built to carry it away. And then, in 1826, Marc Brunel was taken seriously ill, and he had to hand over the building work to his son, Isambard Kingdom Brunel, who was then just twenty years old.

Isambard was to become one of the greatest engineers in history, and the Thames Tunnel was his first big job. Every day water poured into the advancing tunnel, and Isambard had to make the pumps work as hard as they could. But the Tunnel Company started worrying that the work wasn't going fast enough, so they made Isambard move the shield faster than he knew was safe. Also, to try and make more money, they started selling tickets to people who wanted to visit the work. Isambard knew that the river was going to break through, and he hoped that it wouldn't be while the tunnel was full of visitors.

"It's coming in!"

On the night of 18 May 1827, his worst fears came true. The river burst through the roof, and the navvies had to run for their lives from a huge wave which swept through the tunnel. Isambard stood at the bottom of the shaft, urging his men to safety. They ran up the spiral staircase in the shaft as fast as they could. When they got to the top they realized that one man, an old pump operator called Tillet, was still down in the tunnel. Isambard could hear his faint cries for help. At once, he tied a rope round himself, and slid down into the black shaft to

17

find the missing man. Struggling through the rising water, Isambard found Tillet, tied the rope around his waist, and pulled him to safety at the top of the shaft. By a miracle, no one had been killed.

But now the tunnel was full of water. Isambard went down to the bottom of the river, and saw where the Thames had broken in. He decided to try and plug the hole by dropping hundreds of sacks filled with clay and hazel twigs into the river above the tunnel. The work took months. First the hole had to be blocked, then the water had to be pumped out, and then the shield had to cleared of hundreds of tons of mud. By November, Isambard was ready to start digging again, and to celebrate, he arranged a huge banquet in the tunnel. Isambard and his friends sat down with the navvies, and enjoyed a feast under the river, with the band of the Coldstream Guards for entertainment!

Digging started again, but on January 12th 1828 the river burst through once more, even more disastrously than before. Once again, Isambard was down in the tunnel, but this time he was not so lucky. Hearing the water roaring through the tunnel, he started to help two of his men, Ball and Collins, who were caught up in the flood, but his foot was trapped by some fallen timber, and it seemed certain that he could not escape. His assistant, Beamish, waited anxiously at the top of the shaft for Isambard. Realizing that Isambard was in great danger, Beamish fought his way down the steps past the men who were

18

trying to escape upwards. Then, to Beamish's horror, a great wave came surging up the shaft, carrying with it the body of Isambard. At first Beamish was sure that Isambard must be dead, until the engineer started calling for Ball and Collins. Isambard was alive, but badly injured; Ball and Collins and four other navvies were killed.

Now Marc took over again from Isambard, who was too ill to work. He dropped 4500 tons of clay into the river to block up the hole. This cost so much that the Company ran out of money, and the tunnel was bricked up. It seemed that the Brunels had failed. But after seven

years, the government decided to put forward the money to complete the tunnel, and in 1836, work started again. By this time Isambard had recovered from his terrible injuries, but was beginning work on The Great Western Railway, which would make him rich and world famous. So Marc had to take charge without the help of his son. The work was never easy. Water still poured in. The tunnel filled with poisonous gas, and the soft gravel kept sinking and giving way. But Marc knew that his shield would work, and, in 1843, the tunnel was finished at last. Marc was knighted by the Queen for his work, but he died shortly afterwards, worn out.

An underwater journey

You can still go through Marc and Isambard's Thames Tunnel. It's part of the Tube now. It's on one of the shortest Underground lines, the East London Line, which is marked in orange on the Tube map.

The original Thames Tunnel runs from Wapping to Rotherhithe. The best way to travel through it is to start at Wapping Station, where there are some diagrams, plans and drawings of the tunnel on the platform walls. Then take the train for Rotherhithe, through the tunnel. It's only a short ride by fast train, and as you make the journey, remember the great banquet that was held in the tunnel, and hope that the ghosts of the navvies who died while the tunnel was being built aren't sitting in the seat behind you. The roof of the tunnel is so near to the bottom of the river, that if you could stop the train to listen, you would be able to hear noise from the propellers of ships in the river above.

Get out at Rotherhithe. As you walk up towards the station entrance, you are at the bottom of the shaft in which Isambard nearly died. The station is on Brunel Road, named after

Isambard and Marc; turn left out of the station, and walk towards the strange round building about 100 metres away on the right-hand side of the road. This is one of the air shafts of the Rotherhithe Road Tunnel, which begins its journey under the Thames close by. If you visited the Millennium Dome, you might remember one of the air shafts from the Blackwall Tunnel sticking up through the canopy. Without these ventilation shafts, the road tunnels would fill with car fumes, and anyone trying to drive through would be killed.

If you turn around and walk a couple of hundred metres past the station, you can see the entrance to the road tunnel under St Olaf's Square; it was built by the wonderfully named Sir Maurice Fitzmaurice.

If you head back towards the station, and turn up the road beside it, you will quickly come to the Brunel Engine House Museum. The red fence outside guards the mouth to the top of the original shaft. The Engine House is where the pumps which were used to keep the Tunnel clear of water were kept, and you can still see one of the enormous pumping engines in place. There's also an exhibition about the building of the tunnel. It's easy to imagine Isambard in here, urging the firemen to stoke up the fires of the steam pumps to suck out the water from the Tunnel, so that he could begin digging again.

After your visit to the Engine House, get back onto the East London Line and go south. Change onto the Jubilee Line at Canada Water, and head east for Canary Wharf. You've just been under the Thames again, in one of the newest tunnels, finished in 1999. It's worth getting off at Canary Wharf to see the Tube station. This is one of the largest Underground stations in the world. It's truly spectacular, and with luck, people will still be coming to visit it in 150 years, like we can visit Brunel's Engine House today.

If you have time, take the Docklands Light Railway from Canary Wharf towards Lewisham, and get off at Cutty Sark Station. You've just passed under the Thames a third time, in another brand new tunnel. It's still difficult to tunnel under rivers, but what took Marc and Isambard eighteen years to build now only takes a couple of months using modern equipment. Tunnelling engineers still use an up-to-date version of Marc's shield in their work. If you get out at Cutty Sark and walk towards the river, you'll see the dome on the roof of the entry shaft to the Greenwich Foot Tunnel. Take the lift or walk down the spiral stairs for this last journey under the river. As you walk through the spooky corridor, surrounded by echoing voices and footsteps, remember that the Thames is running only a few feet above your head. Watch out for those drips, and hope they don't turn into a flood, or, like Isambard Kingdom Brunel, you might get swept along on a wave to be washed out at the top of the shaft like a bobbing cork.

The tunnels under the Thames (going downriver from Hammersmith Bridge)

1. Water main from Barnes to the Riverside Theatre in Hammersmith.

2. Electric cable tunnel from Battersea Power Station.

3. Hot water tunnel from Battersea Power Station, to carry water for heating the Churchill Gardens Estate. This is not used anymore, since the power station closed, which is a shame. Power stations produce a lot of waste heat, and central heating is a good way to use the waste.

4 and 5. Tunnels carrying the Victoria Line, between Victoria and Pimlico stations.

6. West End branch of the Northern Line, between Waterloo and Embankment.

7. Bakerloo Line, also between Waterloo and Embankment.

8. The Waterloo and City Line, which is known as 'The Drain'.

9. The Northern Line between Bank and London Bridge.

10 and 11. Two tunnels carrying telephone cables, one near Hungerford Bridge, and one under Blackfriars Bridge.

12. Disused Underground line, from London Bridge to King William Street.

13. Tower Subway, which runs under HMS Belfast. This was once a pedestrian tunnel; now it just carries television cables.

14. Marc and Isambard's Thames Tunnel.

15. The Rotherhithe Road Tunnel.

16. Jubilee Line between Canada Water and Canary Wharf.

17. Electrical cable tunnel, between Deptford Power Station and the Isle of Dogs.

18. Docklands Light Railway between Island Gardens and Cutty Sark.

19. The Greenwich Foot Tunnel.

20. The Jubilee Line again, from Canary Wharf to North Greenwich.

21 and 22. The Blackwall Road Tunnels.

23. The Jubilee Line yet again, between North Greenwich and Canning Town.

24. The Woolwich Foot Tunnel.

25. Cable tunnel between Barking Power Station and Thamesmead.

26 and 27. Two service tunnels under the Thames Barrier.

28. The Dartford Tunnel, which takes the M25 under the river, and is the closest tunnel to the sea.

CHAPTER THREE

The Sewers

Have you ever thought about what a city actually is? It's more than a lot of houses, businesses, schools, cinemas, parks and hospitals. You need to move things around, and to provide power. There needs to be clean water, and the streets must be safe from crime. There are hundreds of things that a city needs to do to make it a decent place to live. A city is a machine. And like any machine, a city produces waste. Waste has to be cleaned away, or the machine wouldn't work. A lot of it comes out of us, the people who live in the city. Millions of people make millions of tons of pooh! As long as people have lived together, what to do with their pooh has been a problem.

There were drains and sewers in Roman London. Archaeologists have found clay pipes hidden under the streets. You can see pieces of Roman pipes in the Museum of London. These sewers all emptied into the many rivers of London, which in turn ran down to the Thames. This means that all of the businesses that needed clean water had to be upstream from where the rivers dumped their load of pooh in the Thames. It also means that the richer you were, the higher up the river you lived, because it was much less smelly. But for the Romans, it probably wasn't too much of a problem, because there weren't so many people as there are now.

Flying pooh

As London grew in size, so it grew in stinky nastiness too. The old Roman sewers were lost and buried, and no one seemed to care. In the houses that filled London before the Great Fire of 1666, the top floors where people lived hung out over the street. Before flush toilets came into use, in the early 1800s, people had to

use potties, or chamber pots as they were called. And when they needed emptying, people just emptied them from their windows into the street below. This was not much fun if you were walking by at the time. The person who was emptying their chamber pots used to call '*Gardez l'eau!*', which is French for, 'Look out for the water!', but you can imagine that lots of people didn't hear the warning in time. And even if they did hear the warning, and managed not to get hit, London's streets were disgusting. The pooh fell into an open channel in the middle of the street, which was then supposed to drain down into the rivers. Of course, much of it didn't drain away at all.

In the Middle Ages, the City government began to worry about the problem. People were forced by law to build cesspits, great holes in the ground outside their houses where they threw their pooh. Believe it or not, archaeologists are always very interested when they discover a medieval cesspit. It can tell them a lot about how people used to live. After a time, the cess pits would become full, and would need to be emptied. This was the job of the nightsoilman. Nightsoil was what people politely called pooh. It was such a horrible job that the nightsoilmen were quite well paid. They made money from selling the pooh, as well. It was used in the manufacture of saltpetre, which is an important ingredient in the making of gunpowder. But people realized that cesspits were not good enough, so they started to build underground sewers again, to carry the pooh down to the Thames. Many of the tunnels they built are still in use today.

By the 1800s, these medieval sewers were not up to the job. They were terrible places to work. The tunnels were very narrow and full of disgusting gas. And full of rats. There were

stories of men being eaten alive by rats, stripped down to their skeletons. There were stories too of a race of wild pigs, called sewerswine, who lived in the sewers under Hampstead. No one ever saw one, but the men who worked in the sewer still believed the stories. The rats are still there, even if the pigs have gone. There are probably ten million rats living in London's sewers today. As well as the flushermen, whose job was to clean the sewers, there were lots of men who worked as toshers. They would get into the sewer and rake through the pooh, looking for anything valuable which people had dropped down the loo. Not a very nice job, though a tosher could make lots of money.

The Great Stink

The sewers still emptied into the Thames, just as they had in Roman times, only now there were a great many more people living in London. So the Thames stank. By the 1840s people were very worried about the state of the sewers, and it was decided to clean them out properly. Over 300 sewers were flushed out. Only this made things worse, since all the pooh was washed down into the Thames at once. The river became thick and brown, and any time paddle steamers came up the river, all they did was to stir it up and make it worse. In 1858 London was overcome with 'The Great Stink', when even The House of Commons filled with the most horrible stench. At last something would have to be done.

And the smell was not the biggest problem. In 1849, almost 15,000 people in London died from the terrible water-borne disease cholera. Over 10,000 died in 1854, and 5,500 in 1866. It had taken scientists a long time to find the link between good health and clean water, and finding out meant that it was even more important to work out what should be done with the pooh. An engineer called Joseph Bazalgette came up with the answer.

Bazalgette decided to build six huge underground drains which ran parallel to the river, three on the north side, and three on the south. These drains, rather grandly called interceptory sewers, then carried the pooh away to cleaning stations far downriver. Bazalgette's secret was gravity. He knew that because London is built on gravel terraces, it slopes down towards the Thames, and that the Thames runs down towards the sea. All he had to do was make the tunnels big enough, and then let gravity carry the mess away. Just to make sure, he built some huge pumping stations, one of which, Abbey Mills, in Stratford, you can sometimes visit. From Abbey Mills, the waste was carried to Beckton Water works, where the sewage was cleaned before being released into the Thames. There is another sewer system in South London. The sewers meet the river at Crossness, near Erith, where you can see the old pumping engines, and even visit a toilet museum! Bazalgette's system grew all through the nineteenth century, and was so successful, that by 1896, there were no cases of cholera in the whole of London.

The sewerman's fear of the rain storm

Cleaning sewers is probably not the greatest job in the world, but at least today the workers have closed circuit television to help them find blockages and leaks. They still have to get down and dig out the blockages by hand, though. One of the biggest

problems they face is congealed fat
from restaurants. That's why you
shouldn't put fat down the sink!
The biggest danger they face is a
sudden rainstorm. The
drains can fill very
quickly, and the
workers can easily
be drowned. One of
the sewer gang always stays
above the ground to alert the underground workers if it starts
to rain, so that they can escape before the tunnels
start to fill up.

It's difficult to arrange a visit to a sewer. Although you can
visit sewers in Paris and Brighton, it is very rare that Thames
Water allows visitors down into London's vast network. There
are over 700 miles of main sewer drain. Perhaps they are
worried that people might get lost, or get attacked by rats or
wild pigs. But you can walk along the top of one of Bazalgette's
interceptory sewers. Start by visiting his statue, which is right
by Hungerford Railway Bridge, near Charing Cross Station, and
then turn and walk along the Victoria Embankment towards the
City. Bazalgette built the Victoria Embankment to carry one of
his great drains. The pooh you had yesterday could be running
right under your feet. The Thames has been getting cleaner
each year, thanks to Joseph Bazalgette and his sewers. As you

look over the wall of the Embankment into the river, think about what it must have been like in the year of The Great Stink, and about all the lives that were saved, just by building proper drains. Joseph Bazalgette deserves his statue – he is one of London's greatest heroes.

The story of a pooh

Straight after I came out into the light, I was dropped into a pool of water. Luckily, I am a good swimmer, but I was a bit fed up when someone dropped a load of soggy paper onto my head. Still, the pool seemed a nice place, with high white sides. I floated there for a few moments, wondering what would happen next, when I heard a great roaring sound, and gallons of water came pouring down the sides of the pool. Before I knew what was happening, I was sucked under the water, and started falling and tumbling down a long black pipe, until I landed with a bump in a dark narrow tunnel. I was very frightened, but before I had time to think, I realized that there was a trickle of water in the tunnel, which ran slightly downhill, and that I was floating again.

Now began a strange time. I floated down the little tunnel, past lots of big rats, and dropped into another tunnel, a little bigger than the first. Other tunnels emptied into this one, and I was joined by other poohs, just like me. Then, just as I was becoming comfortable, I was flushed into another, even bigger tunnel, where the water flowed quite fast. This was exciting, as I whizzed along in the stream, and I was just beginning to enjoy myself, when I stuck fast on a big heap of hard fat. This was not very nice, and I was stuck there for days. Suddenly I saw lights, and heard voices, and I was very pleased when a gang of men came wading up the tunnel, and started to dig away the fat. I was unstuck, and was washed back into the stream. With a great bump, I fell into the biggest tunnel I had ever seen, with very fast flowing water, and thousands of rats. I turned over and over in the water, and my journey continued for days, until at last, I came out into the light again, to find myself in another huge pool. That is where I am now, with lots of other poohs. The others tell me that we are in a slurry pond at Crossness Sewage Works, and that when we have sunk to the bottom, all the water will be sucked away for cleaning, and we will be turned into fertilizer. Then we will be spread over fields, to help crops grow. And that then, someone will eat the crops, and my strange journey in the dark will begin all over again.

CHAPTER FOUR

Underground Rivers

If you have ever stood on the edge of a gravelly beach, where the stones meet the sand, you will know that lots of small streams run out of the gravel, over the sand and down to the sea. Since London is made in the same way as a gravel beach, you would expect there to be streams and rivers running down from the heights towards the river. There are a few rivers in London - the Lea in the east, the Wandle in the south, and the Brent in the west - which are still open as they run down to the Thames. But you might expect many more. London used to have lots of rivers and streams, over a hundred miles of them. But now they are almost all buried, deep underground. Sometimes it is difficult to know where the rivers flow, or even if they existed at all. They have become lost rivers. But, if you look and listen, you can follow the course of London's underground rivers yourself.

Where is the Walbrook?

In the Middle Ages, the first man to write about London was William Fitzstephens, and he said that London was lucky because of its excellent springs with 'water sweet and clear'. But by the 1500s, when London started to grow outside the old Roman walls, London's streams had become filthy and polluted sewers, and people started building over them. One of the first to disappear was the Walbrook, which flowed through the City of London. Just to show how lost some of these rivers really are, people are still arguing about where the source of the Walbrook was. Some people say it was in Islington, or Hoxton; others say that these are just guesses, and that no one really knows at all. We do know that the Walbrook was an important stream for the Romans, and that they built the Temple of Mithras next to it. By the end of the Middle Ages, it had gone. Those who had houses next to it were ordered to pave over the Walbrook, and it became the first lost river of London. The water is still there. The stream was rediscovered during the building of the Bank of England in 1803, and you can still see where the water comes out of a pipe and enters the Thames, by Cannon Street Station.

Walking down the Westbourne

There are some rivers, like the Cranbourn or the Shoreditch, that have been built and covered over for so long, that no one knows for sure where they ran at all. It's only from old maps that historians can begin to work out where they were. But there are other rivers that were covered over quite recently, and if you take an A–Z map book out with you, you can follow their courses. One of the most interesting is the Westbourne. It starts on Hampstead Heath, at the Whitestone Ponds, and goes underground straight away. It crosses Finchley Road and Kilburn High Road, goes under the Grand Union Canal, the Westway and the mainline railway by Paddington station, and makes its way to Hyde Park. This upper part of the river was only built over in the 1830s; it is strange to imagine, standing in the busy streets around Paddington Station, that once people came here to fish.

In Hyde Park, you can actually get in a boat and follow the Westbourne. The river was dammed in 1730 to make the Serpentine boating lake. It used to be crossed here by a bridge, the Knight's Bridge, which has given its name to this part of London. It was a favourite spot for highwaymen to steal from travellers. The river runs under Knightsbridge and Chelsea, and actually crosses the Tube's District Line at Sloane Square Station in a huge pipe. If you stand on the platform and listen carefully, you can sometimes hear the water running above your head. After that, the river divided in two to meet the Thames.

One branch comes out of a pipe between Chelsea Bridge and the Embankment Gardens, and the other was used to make the old Grosvenor Canal, which you can still see as you pull out of Victoria station.

Floating down the Fleet

The most famous and important river of London after the Thames was the Fleet. Although by the time it was finally covered over in the 1840s it was nothing more than a filthy sewer, it had been a wide water road, right up through the heart of London. It has its beginnings on Hampstead Heath, like the Westbourne. One of the sources is by Kenwood House, and the other is above the pond by the Vale of Health. You will need your boots if you want to find this source. This is where the sand of the Heath meets the London clay, and there are many tiny springs which feed the pond. It can be very muddy, but unless it has been raining, you will not see running water. But if you walk down the Heath from pond to pond, you can follow the Fleet. It's not always easy to push your way through the bushes to find this tiny muddy brook running between the ponds, but it is exciting. After the last pond, the Fleet goes underground to continue its journey down to the Thames. It meets the branch from Kenwood House just north of Camden Town Tube station. The Fleet was once sixteen feet wide here, and an anchor was found in the bed of the river, so it is possible that boats used to come this far up the from the Thames. The Fleet now runs down Pancras Way towards Kings Cross. Pancras Way was once known as Pancras Wash. A river wash is a piece of land which is often flooded after rain, so it is possible that the Fleet often came over its banks here. Once again, old street names give us clues about the secret world buried beneath our feet.

The Fleet runs between Farringdon Road and Gray's Inn Road, and if you look carefully, you can see that you are in a valley, even today. During the English Civil War of the 1640s when the forces of King Charles I and those of Parliament were fighting fierce battles all across England, London was held by the Parliamentary (or Roundhead) army. It was always under threat from the King's Army, and the Fleet was a very important line of defence. Mounds of earth were thrown up all along the riverbanks to stop London from being attacked. As you walk down Farringdon Road, try to imagine the Roundhead soldiers standing guard, waiting for the King's Army to attack. By Farringdon Tube station, you can find Turnmill Street. The Turnmill was another name for the Fleet. This was because the river was lined with watermills, which used the power of the water to grind corn into flour. Several other streams once joined the Fleet. One, which was called the Faggeswell Brook,

flowed into the Fleet from the meat market at Smithfield, and it was supposed to run red with blood.

Another was known as the Old Bourne, and it was from this stream (or 'bourne') that we get the name Holborn today. Blood was not the worst of the things that flowed into the Fleet. Londoners treated it as an open sewer, and it was stinking and filthy. So, like the Walbrook, it was slowly covered and built over. Until the Great Fire of London in 1666, there were still wharves on the Fleet, where barges unloaded coal from Newcastle, but when London was rebuilt after the Fire, the wharves were not rebuilt, and most of the river was covered over. Sir Christopher Wren, the great architect who rebuilt the City, turned the lower part of the Fleet into a canal, but even this did not clean it up, and still Londoners continued to pollute their river. Poets of the early 1700s wrote about the filthy Fleet. Jonathon Swift wrote that the river was full of *'seepings from butchers stalls, dung, guts and blood,*

Drowned puppies, stinking sprats, all drenched in mud...'

The poet Alexander Pope wrote in the 1720s that the Fleet

'rolls a large tribute of dead dogs to Thames'

It smelt so badly that in 1765 the lower part of the river was finally arched over, and most people forgot that there had ever been a river running through London at all.

But they were reminded in the 1830s when the river tunnels became so full of stinking gas that they exploded. At King's Cross the road became unusable, and three houses in Clerkenwell were swept away in a huge wave of pooh! The Fleet still had its uses, even though it was buried in tunnels, and Joseph Bazelgette used it when he was building his great system of sewers, to help flush out the tunnels. Even today, when it has been raining, you can see what's left of the Fleet, coming out into the Thames from the mouth of a pipe by Blackfriars Bridge. London has changed since William Fitzstephens praised it for its 'waters sweet and clear'!

How to find an underground river.

If you look in the back of the A–Z book, you will find lots of streets named after the Westbourne, which will help you to follow its course. They are (take a deep breath!):

Westbourne Avenue, Westbourne Bridge, Westbourne Crescent, Westbourne Gardens, Westbourne Grove, Westbourne Grove Terrace, Westbourne House, Westbourne Park, Westbourne Park Passage, Westbourne Park Road, Westbourne Park Villas, Westbourne Place, Westbourne Road, Westbourne Street, and Westbourne Terrace! Or you could just find Fleet Street!

CHAPTER FIVE

Underground Railways

London's Underground Railway, known as the Tube, has been in the news since the first part was opened in the 1860s. Governments and councils are always trying to find ways to make it better. Passengers think that the people who are running it could do a much better job. For the millions of people who use it every year to get to work or school and to the shops, it is very important that the Tube trains are fast and frequent. But for the dedicated underground explorer, the Tube can be a strange and fascinating world to discover.

The world's first underground railway

There are so many things to see and places to visit on the Tube. There are 287 stations on twelve different lines, which spread all across London. A good place to start is the London Transport Museum in Covent Garden. Here you can find out all about the history of the Underground and sit in some of the old trains. The first part of London's Underground to open was the Metropolitan Railway in 1863 between Paddington and Farringdon. This was the world's first underground railway and it took three years to build. The method that the engineers used was called cut and cover. The builders cut up the roads, built a huge trench in which they lay the railway line, covered it over with arches and then rebuilt the road over the top. The sewer railway, as it was known, was a huge success, even though it was very filthy. Special steam engines pulled the trains, which were supposed to be much cleaner than ordinary engines, but still the tunnels quickly became full of soot. Business people saw the success of the Metropolitan Line, and they started to build other lines until by the beginning of the 20th century they had all joined together, and the Circle was completed.

After the First World War many more new lines were built, but now deep under ground, using modern versions of Marc Brunel's tunnelling shield. Although this way of building underground railways is very expensive, it stops roads being dug up and buildings knocked down, which had been the case with cut and cover. When you explore the Tube system it is important to

remember that it was the world's first underground railway.
Although Londoners are proud they were first, it means that
London's Tube is also very old and in need of repair.

Going
underground

An all-zones travelcard and a
tube map are all you really
need to explore the railway.
The different lines are
marked on the map in
different colours, and the
stations where you can
change from one line to
another are marked with a
circle. The map is not much
help if you are travelling

overground. It does not show the way the lines really run or how
far apart the stations are. If it did, it would be much more
complicated to use. The first Underground maps were drawn
showing all the twists and turns that the lines take. In the
1920s a man called Harry Beck realized this did not help
passengers, but just made the map confusing, and he designed
the map that we see today. Because the map does not show how
far apart the stations are, visitors to London often get caught
out. The shortest distance between stations is that between

Leicester Square and Covent Garden on the Piccadilly Line, at just 0.16 miles. It is much quicker and easier to walk than to take the Tube; but it is the most popular journey taken by tourists!

Another good place to start exploring the Tube from is Baker Street Station. It was part of the original line and if you stand on the Circle Line platform you can see how cut and cover worked and how shallow the lines are. The beautiful brickwork of the the arches have recently been cleaned and restored but are otherwise unchanged since the 1860s. Then you can walk through to the platforms where the Metropolitan Line runs out to the far suburbs and take the escalator down to the deep-level Tube lines of the Bakerloo and the Jubilee. The Jubilee Line extension from Westminster to Stratford was only finished in 1999 and was the world's most expensive railway line ever built, at £330 million per mile.

The new stations are well worth visiting, especially Canary Wharf, Canada Water and North Greenwich. The Tube has always tried to make its stations modern and attractive, and the Piccadilly Line has lots of interesting buildings from the 1930s, like the station at Arnos Grove. Lots of the original stations were covered in red tiles. Many of them are still in use, like the one at Maida Vale, though you should look out for the wind which whistles through the tunnels here. These old tiled stations offer us clues to where a station has been rebuilt or abandoned, as sections of the buildings can remain even when the station has become disused. There are more than thirty abandoned or ghost stations. A famous one is the old British Museum station between Holborn and Tottenham Court Road on the Central Line. Keep your eyes open and you might spot the old tiles from the platform walls.

Passengers on the Piccadilly Line were surprised recently when their train stopped in the darkness of a tunnel, and the famous actor and comedian Billy Connolly got on. He had been making a film in one of the abandoned stations, Down Street, and asked that a train stop at the old station to pick him up. Nobody on the train knew that there had once been a station there!

There are blocked-up lines too. Until quite recently you could travel between Holborn and Aldwych: now Aldwych station is abandoned and the line is closed. One of the strange things about the Underground is how much of it is above-ground – just over half of the 257 miles of line! There used to be even more, as the above-ground Underground stretched right out into the countryside. The District Line ran to Windsor and the Metropolitan stretched as far as Aylesbury, but now these lines have been abandoned too.

The Tube is famous for its escalators. There are 409 of them. Every week they go round and round for thousands of miles, as far as two trips around the world! The first escalator was built at Earl's Court in 1911. The early escalators were made of wood and at first people were worried about using them. A man with a wooden leg was employed to travel up and down all day to show that it was safe. If you like escalators, Bank has more than any other station: fifteen, and two moving walkways. The longest

escalator, not just in the Tube system, but in the whole of Europe, is at Angel. The shortest is at Chancery Lane station. At Bank, by the platform for the Waterloo and City line, there is a 'travellator', which is a kind of sloping escalator without steps.

Sometimes Underground stations have lifts instead of escalators. The deepest lift shaft, at 191 feet, is at Hampstead on the Northern Line. Unsurprisingly this line is also the deepest on the Tube system. As it goes under Hampstead Heath, it is over 220 feet below the surface.

The longest continuous run on the Tube system is from Epping to West Ruislip on the Central Line. It is 34 miles long. The shortest line is the Waterloo and City: it has only two stations and is just two miles long.

If you buy a day travelcard, you can get around all day and not spend very much money. But there is one underground train journey you can make for free. The Heathrow Express, which runs modern trains non-stop from Paddington to Heathrow Airport, usually costs about fourteen pounds for a fifteen-minute journey. But if you get on at Terminal Three, you can ride to Terminal Four for nothing. The journey only lasts four minutes. But you can sit back in the luxurious seats, and even watch a video, and for those few minutes, you can imagine that you're about to fly away to some faraway place. The only problem is, how to get to Heathrow for your free ride? The best way, of course, is by Tube. And for that you need a travelcard!

Pigeons and poltergeists

The strangest passengers are the pigeons. Often you can see pigeons getting on and off the trains. There is a story that pigeons looking for food travel from East London up to the West End by Tube to save their wings! There are other animals down there, too, especially rats and mice. Oxford Circus is a good place to see mice scurrying about on the line, quite unconcerned about the trains running inches away from their heads.

The Tube can be a mysterious place at night... The trains do not run long after midnight, but the tunnels are still full of people. Engineers and train maintenance workers stay up all night to make sure that the trains run safely in the morning.

49

One very important group of night workers are the fluffers. They work very hard to keep the tunnels and lines free from fluff which can stop the trains and is a fire risk. But down in the dark tunnels at night, the fluffers can sometimes see strange things.

Bank Station is haunted by the ghost of the Black Nun. Her brother was a cashier at the Bank of England and he was hanged for forging bank notes. His sister waited outside the bank for him for forty years, until she died. Now her ghost wanders the platforms of the stations, waiting for a brother who will never come.

Covent Garden is haunted by a man in old-fashioned clothes and a top hat and at Farringdon people say that they sometimes hear terrible screams echo through the tunnels. The fluffers call the ghost the Screeching Spectre.

Most frightening of all are the legends about a terrible race of monsters who live in the Tube network. The story is that the monsters are descended from workers who were trapped alive during the building of the lines and that now, after a hundred years, they grab unsuspecting passengers and eat them. They have lost nearly all their powers of speech and all they can say now is, "Mind the doors!"

As you explore London's fascinating Tube network, you will have to decide for yourself whether this story is true or not ... but be careful!

Underground facts and figures

More than two million people use the Underground every day.

The District Line is the busiest, carrying 180 million passengers per year.

The highest point reached by the Underground is Amersham station, on the Metropolitan Line. It is 500 feet above sea level.

The least underground part of the Underground is the Dolly Brook Viaduct on the Mill Hill East branch of the Northern Line, which carries the line 60 feet over the road below.

The longest journey completely underground is from Morden to

East Finchley, on the City Branch of the Northern Line; it is over seventeen miles long.

The busiest stations are Victoria and Oxford Circus. Both are used by 85 million travellers a year.

The biggest station is at Baker Street, which has ten platforms. Moorgate also has ten platforms, but four of them are used by Thameslink Trains, and not London Underground.

There are three stations which have only one platform; Heathrow Terminal Four on the Piccadilly, Chesham on the Metropolitan, and Mill Hill East on the Northern.

The longest gap between stations is between Chesham and Chalfont and Latimer, at over four miles.

There are different kinds of train carriages on all the different lines. The tunnels were all built to different widths, and so a train that runs on the Bakerloo Line, for example, would not fit into the Piccadilly Line tubes. See how many different kinds of train you can spot.

The Tube in a day – a puzzle

They said it couldn't be done. All my friends told me I was mad.
But as a dedicated Underground explorer, I wanted to prove
them wrong. My plan was to travel on every single line on the
London Underground in just one day! I sat down with a Tube map
(which are free at all the stations) and planned my route,
starting from my local station, Highbury and Islington, which is
on the Victoria Line. The first train heading north left at a
quarter to six in the morning, and I was almost still asleep as I
climbed aboard to make my marathon journey.

I stayed on the train when we got to Walthamstow Central,
and travelled back down the line to Brixton; then back from
Brixton, and changed at Stockwell for the Northern Line. The
Northern Line has lots of branches. First, I travelled south to
Morden, and then north again, for High Barnet, via the Charing
Cross Branch. At High Barnet I got on another train going south,
and changed at Finchley Central for the short branch to Mill Hill
East. It seemed strange to think that I was supposed to be on
an Underground train, because much of this branch is carried
high on viaducts and embankments above the houses. Back on
the train again, heading south for Camden, I changed onto the
Edgware branch, and headed right out into the north of London.
Then back to Bank, on the City Branch, where I got onto a
Central Line train, heading for Epping. Right at the end of the
Central line, it's hard to tell that you are still in the city, as the
line runs through woods and fields. After Epping, I changed at

Woodford, and got onto what is called 'The Fairlop Loop', which took me back to Bank. At Bank, I just had time to get onto the Waterloo and City, and back again, before hopping back onto the Northern Line, heading south again. At Elephant and Castle I got onto the Bakerloo, which took me up to Harrow and Wealdstone. Then I got off and walked to Harrow-on-the-Hill station, on the Metropolitan Line (it's only about half a mile). From there I went to Amersham, then back to Chalfont and Latimer for the branch to Chesham. I got a train at Chesham that was going all the way back into London, but I got off at Moor Park, and took the Watford branch. From Watford I went back to Harrow-on-the-Hill, and changed again for the line to Uxbridge. (I'm getting out of breath here!) At Uxbridge, I got onto a Piccadilly Line train and then changed at Acton Town for the line out to Heathrow. You can stay on at Heathrow, because the line doesn't end, but loops back on itself. Then I went all the way back into the West End, and changed at Green Park for the Jubilee Line, which took me to Canada Water, where I got onto an East London Line train. A quick trip through Brunel's tunnel, change at Whitechapel onto the District Line, and back to Victoria station, where I got onto the Victoria Line again. The ride back to Highbury and Islington seemed to take hours! I got back to my starting stayion just after midnight, eighteen and a half hours after I had set off.

My friends were right. I must be mad. But the puzzle is this: had I managed to get right round the whole Tube system? And if not, what parts had I missed out? See if you can follow my trip on your Tube map. And see if you can work out a way to do the whole Tube system in just one day.

CHAPTER SIX

War under London

The tunnels and caves of London were never more useful than during the Second World War. The United Kingdom went  to war with Nazi Germany in September 1939 because the Nazis were trying to take over Europe. They had already invaded Czchekoslovakia, in 1938. When they invaded Poland, in 1939, the British and French governments declared war. For the first few months of the war, nothing much seemed to be happening, but in 1940 the Nazi leader Adolf Hitler sent his troops through Holland and Belgium into France, which he quickly conquered. The United Kingdom was the last place in Europe to hold out against the Nazi advance. Many people in the UK, including many in Parliament, wanted to let the Nazis keep Europe, if they would let the British keep their Empire. But the British Prime Minister, Winston Churchill, insisted that the Nazis must be fought, whatever the cost. And so Hitler turned his bombers on British towns and cities. London was the worst hit of all. Half a million homes were destroyed by bombs during the war, and one and a half million were badly damaged.

Blitzed!

Between September 1940 and May 1941, tens of thousands of bombs were dropped on London. This period is known as the 'Blitz'. On just one night, 15 October 1940, 410 Nazi bombers dropped 538 tons of high explosive, killing 400 citizens of London, and seriously injuring 900 more. Almost a thousand fires were started all over London. That much high explosive could have killed up to 25,000 people. But it did not because Londoners had gone underground into bomb shelters, basements and, most famously, the Tube.

Those Londoners who were lucky enough to have a garden could build their own shelter. These were known as Anderson shelters, after the government minister who decided that everyone who wanted one could have one free. They were not built very far underground. If you wanted to build one, you had to dig a hole, 3 feet deep. Then you put the Anderson shelter into the ground. They were made of two curved sheets of corrugated iron, bolted together, which were then covered over with the earth that had been dug out from the hole. Many people planted vegetables on top of their shelters! They could hold up to six people, most uncomfortably, especially if you tried to sleep, as they did not keep out the terrible noise of the bombs. Also, these shallow shelters often flooded, and they would have to be baled out like a boat before they could be used.

Here and there across London there are a few Anderson

shelters left, and you can see one that has been built in the Imperial War Museum.

Those Londoners who didn't have gardens had to find other underground places to hide. Early on in the war, the Government decided that they didn't want to build deep underground shelters, in case people just went and hid instead of going to work. At first, they built above-ground shelters, but these were very unpopular. People started to find their own underground dens. Many people hid in the crypts of churches. There were basements all over London where people hid. One of the best known was called 'Mickey's Shelter', a huge underground warehouse in Stepney that could hold as many as 5,000 people. It was run by Mickey Davis, who was just 3 feet and 6 inches tall. That didn't stop him trying to make sure that the shelter was as well run as possible.

Other people took over Chislehurst Caves, just outside London, in Kent. No one is quite sure how the caves came to be here, but it is most likely that they are ancient mines. As news of how comfortable and safe the caves were spread throughout London, more and more people turned up each night. During the worst of the Blitz, special trains used to run from London every evening, carrying hundreds of people who wanted to spend the night in the caves. The railway company often had to put up signs at the station saying that the caves were full. Grown-ups were charged a penny to get in, and children were let in free. So many people turning up meant that the Caves had to be carefully organized. They were divided into areas for shopping, washing and sleeping. The sleeping areas were known as dormitory sections, and each family was given a 'pitch' to sleep in. There were strict rules if you wanted to stay in Chuislehurst Caves. Here are just some of them:

- No admission or re-entry to the Dormitory Section after 9.30 p.m.

- Pitches must be kept clean

- Unauthorized sale of goods is prohibited

- Lights out and absolute silence by 10.30 p.m. in the Dormitory Section

- Pitches must not be changed, exchanged, or sold

- Four days' absence may involve loss of pitch

- Music must cease by 9 p.m.

- Arrive early and stay put!

Although it might sound strict, people were very happy to get a pitch in the caves. There were electric lights and toilets, as well as bunk beds and proper places to wash. By the end of the war there were shops, churches, a barber's shop, a dance hall and a gym down in the Caves. There was even a hospital, and a baby was born deep underground; her parents called her Cavina! Some people wanted to stay after the end of the war, because it was so comfortable. They were not allowed, but you can still visit Chislehurst Caves today.

Down in the Tube station at midnight

Not surprisingly, people came to see the deep-level Tube lines as the best place to spend the night. The Government disagreed. They didn't want the stations full of sleeping people. So they put up signs at the stations saying, 'Passengers Only during Air Raids'. People just started buying the cheapest tickets they could, and staying down in the tunnels all night. One night, it was worked out that 177,000 people were sleeping down in the Tube tunnels. They were very crowded, and families struggled to find a space on the platforms where they could sleep. After the trains stopped running, and the electricity was turned off, people would sling hammocks over the line. In some stations, people would bring musical instruments, and there would be singing. In others, people would hold debates about books or politics.

Children often enjoyed sleeping down in the tunnels. They ate all the chocolate bars from the machines, and rode on the escalators and trains. But the Tube stations were horrible places at night. Imagine the sound of thousands of snoring people! Because most of the stations were built below the sewers, there was nowhere for people to wash or go to the toilet. There was pooh everywhere, and the tunnels stank of wee. Several people died from diseases they caught down in the Tube.

The Tube wasn't always safe from bombs, either. If you leant against the wall of the platform, you could sometimes feel vibration from the bombs exploding overhead. Twenty people were killed in the subway at Marble Arch station when an exploding bomb turned the tiles on the wall into deadly splinters. A bomb burst a water main above Balham station on the Northern Line. Water flooded the platforms, and 600 people were drowned. In January 1941, a bomb bounced down the escalator at Bank station, and rolled onto the platform before it exploded, killing 111 sleepers.

But people felt safe in the Tube, and the government decided to make things better for the underground sleepers. They closed off the branch line from Holborn to Aldwych, and gave it over to the shelterers. There was a half-finished tunnel leading out of Liverpool Street station, and that too became a shelter. Chemical toilets were put in the stations, and thousands of bunk beds were installed. Rich people never had to sleep in the Tubes. Posh hotels like the Savoy and the Dorchester had their own underground shelters and restaurants. Some people didn't think this was fair, and one night a demonstration was held. Over a hundred East Enders burst into the Savoy and demanded to be given shelter. As the war went on, it was decided to build proper deep-level shelters. Eight of these were built underneath Tube stations, each holding up to 8,000 people, and four of them were open to the public. (The others were for soldiers.) It is still possible to find several of them today, from the buildings at the top of the ventilation shafts. There is one at Belsize Park, and another at Goodge Street.

It wasn't just people who needed protection during the war. A great city like London is full of works of art, and the government was worried that they would be destroyed by Nazi bombs. So a huge gallery was built deep underground in the Manod slate quarry, near Blaenau Festiniog in Wales, and all of the pictures from the National Gallery on Trafalgar Square were stored there during the war. There were five galleries, each with a huge steel door, and armed guards stood outside the galleries day and night.

And it wasn't just pictures which were hidden in the mine. The Crown Jewels were taken from the Tower of London, and hidden there too. The government was worried that a Nazi commando raid might be organized to steal them! Other treasures were hidden down in the Tube. The famous Elgin Marbles were taken from the British Museum, and hidden on the branch line to Aldwych. The government still maintains the galleries in Wales, in case there is another war.

Winston underground

The wartime prime minister, Winston Churchill, had always believed that deep-level shelters were important. He knew that if the United Kingdom was to stand up to the Nazi bombing, then life must continue as normally as possible. Offices must stay open, and the Government must continue with its work. There had to be somewhere that generals and politicians could meet in safety. And so much of Churchill's work was done in a specially built bunker under the 'New Public Offices', on the corner of Horseguards Parade and Great George Street. This bunker was a closely guarded secret until the 1980s, when it was restored and opened as a museum, called the Cabinet War Rooms. It is a fascinating place to visit. When Churchill was first taken to see the bunker, he said, 'These are the rooms from which I shall direct the war.'

True to his word, there is everything down in the bunker

which could keep Churchill in touch with his generals. There is a specially designed room where the Cabinet would meet and make decisions about how the war was to be run, and a huge map room, where all the information from around the world was gathered, so that Churchill could follow how the war was going. The bunker had its own electric power plant, and even a radio studio from where Churchill could make the broadcasts which were so important throughout the war.

Below the bunker there was a cramped and horrible sleeping area, called the Dock, where the secretaries and soldiers who were working in the bunker could rest. Churchill had his own bedroom, and you can see it today, just at it would have been throughout the war years, the walls covered with maps.

There was just one thing that was missing, and that was a proper flush toilet. Those who were hidden in this most secret shelter had to use smelly chemical loos, just like the people down in the Tube. But there was one room that was always kept locked, and which only the Prime Minister used. The people who worked in the bunker were sure that this was a proper toilet for his private needs. It was only after the war that it was discovered that this most secret room of all was home to a private Transatlantic telephone, which Churchill used to call the American president. When you visit the Cabinet War Rooms, imagine what it must have been like to work down here, and to sleep in the Dock. And imagine how much worse it must have been, down in the Tube, trying to sleep as London was pounded by bombs.

War in the disused stations

The disused underground stations became very useful during the Second World War. The old Down Street station on the Piccadilly Line, which had closed in 1932, was reopened as the headquarters of the officers in charge of all Britain's railways during the war. Churchill visited these important underground rooms, which were 70 feet underground, and described them as being 'a considerable underground office'. Dover Street, which is now part of Green Park Station, became the underground headquarters of London Transport. Brompton Road, also on the Piccadilly was a vital control centre for the Air-Raid Protection wardens. After the war, it was taken over by the Territorial Army (as Britain's part-time soldiers are known), and they still use it today. The deepest ghost station is Bull and Bush, under Hampstead Heath. The station was never finished, and trains never stopped here, but it was used in the war as an army headquarters.

There was even a whole line that was taken over. A 3-mile section of the Central Line which was being built between Leytonsone and Gants Hill but had not yet opened for trains, was turned into a factory for making aircraft parts.

Secret passages

Lots of England's oldest houses have secret passages. Some of them were built for smuggling, and others to hide Catholic priests during the Civil War, when it was a crime to be a Catholic. Sadly, London seems to have very few. There is a private staircase at Hampton Court, which Henry the Eighth used to slip out from his office and into the garden for a breath of fresh air, but that is hardly secret. At the Tower of London, you can see the blocked-up entrance to a sally port. Sally ports were secret tunnels with hidden doors which could be used if a castle was under siege. There is one at Windsor Castle too, which was used during the war to store some of the castle's treasures; the Queen is supposed to have used this tunnel as an air-raid shelter during the war.

There are still some tunnels that are so secret that no one has been able to find them. There is supposed to be a secret passage in Greenwich Hospital which King Charles II used to visit his girlfriend Nell Gwynne at night, but no one has ever found it. No one has ever found the cave in Epping Forest which the notorious highwayman Dick Turpin used as his secret lair. But the most secret passages of all are the ones under the Secret Service buildings in London. People are fairly sure that they are there; but what they are used for, and where they lead, only a British secret agent could tell you. And they're not talking!

Chapter Seven

Pipes and Tunnels, Cables and Caves

London is like an iceberg. The part of London that we can see, above ground, hides a huge network of abandoned buildings, tunnels, pipes, caves and crypts which lies hidden under our feet. In such a vast and ancient city, we only have time to glimpse a tiny part of this world. So here's a lightning tour around some of the parts of hidden London which we have not yet uncovered.

Water and gas go underground

Standing in Piccadilly Circus Tube station, which is cleverly hidden under the statue of Eros, you might be surprised to know that there is another important meeting place for an even deeper system of tunnels under your feet. The water and gas mains for the whole of Central London are carried in eleven miles of specially built subways. As London has grown, so has its need for water. In the Middle Ages, people were still using rivers like the Fleet and the Walbrook for their water. As the rivers became filthy and sewers were bricked over, it was not possible to drink the river water, so fresh water had to piped into London. In the 1500s, the Fleet was dammed to form

Hampstead Ponds, and some of London's water came from there. But there was never enough. The New River, which was finished in 1610, brought water 30 miles from the chalk springs of Hertfordshire right into the heart of London. Much of it is still above ground, but where it goes underground, near Stoke Newington, there is a wonderful pumping station, which looks like a creepy castle.

Most of London's water today comes from the huge reservoirs in West London, near Teddington. It is carried in a huge new pipe, 50 miles long, called the London Ring Water Main. It is the deepest tunnel in London. It carries 300 million gallons of water a day, and is built under the higher ground on the edge of London, so that the water flows down into Central London through the smaller water pipes. The pumping stations are deep under ground. There is one hidden under the Shepherd's Bush roundabout. One pumping station you can visit is at Kew Bridge. You can see the steam engine working, and find out more about where London's water comes from.

The gas mains often share the tunnels with the water mains. Nowadays we use gas for cooking and heating, but in the 1800s the gas was mostly used for lighting. Streets and shops and the houses of well-off people were all lit by gas. London must have looked very different at night from how it does today, in the soft gas light. If you go to the Middle and Inner Temples, in the Inns of Court, you can find the only place in London which is still lit by gas. But beware! This is the light by which Jack the Ripper stalked his victims, and Sherlock Holmes solved his crimes.

All London's electricity runs underground. (See if you can spot the electricity substation in Leicester Square.) So do its telephone lines and television and computer cables. A modern city couldn't work without underground wires. Before the telephone was invented, people sent messages along telegraph wires using Morse Code. The telegraph was invented at about the same time as the railways were being built. The first person to make the telegraph work in a useful way was Isambard Kingdom Brunel. When he stopped working on the Thames Tunnel, he started work on The Great Western Railway, which was to run from London to Bristol. The first working telegraph ran its wires under the railway from Paddington to West Drayton, and the telegraph quickly became very important to the new railways. Now thousands of miles of cable snake their way under our feet, helping more and more people to get in touch with each other. Luckily, we don't need Morse Code anymore.

The world's biggest train-set

There is another electric railway under London apart from the Tube. This one is run by the Post Office, and you can't travel on it unless you are a letter or a parcel. The driverless trains carry mail between Liverpool Street and Paddington Stations, and are linked to all the major post offices in London. The lines meet under Mount Pleasant Post Office. There are shunting tunnels, a depot where the trains are kept and repair workshops deep under the huge Post Office building there. If you are in that part of London, you might try and find the grassy mound where Amwell Street meets the Pentonville Road. This is an underground water tank now, but until a hundred years ago, there was a mysterious cave, known as Merlin's Cave.

Merlin was the magician to King Arthur. It was Merlin who helped Arthur pull the sword from the stone, which showed that he was the true King of all Britain. Arthur had many enemies, and he needed Merlin's help. But Merlin fell under the spell of a mysterious enchantress called Nimue, who sent him to sleep and hid him in a cave. People say that he sleeps there still, until the day when King Arthur comes again, as the legends say he will. If the cave really was Merlin's Cave, he's not there now. There are many other places in Britain which have a Merlin's cave of their own, but you can still find Merlin Street, not far away down Amwell Street.

Another tunnel, which will be the most expensive ever made, is being built under this part of London today. This will carry the new fast rail-link from St Pancras to the Channel Tunnel. It will not be finished for many years, but when it is, trains will rush under London at over 100 miles an hour. The cellars of St Pancras have always been important. The columns which you see supporting the roof go deep into the ground, and are spaced the width of a beer barrel apart.

One of the main cargoes that came into St Pancras was beer from Burton-on-Trent, in the Midlands. It was unloaded straight from the trains into the specially designed cellars, which are still there, under the platforms. The Tube is growing too. Plans have just been made for a new part of the East London Line to open from Shoreditch to Dalston Central. So the newest part of the Tube will be linked to the oldest, Brunel's incredible tunnel under the Thames. In the middle of Kingsway, you can see all that is left of a failed experiment to carry trams under London. Trams are a cross between buses and trains. They run through the street on rails. A new tram system has just

opened in Croydon, but above ground. Somebody had the bright idea to make the trams run in special tunnels, but the idea never caught on, and the old tunnel in Kingsway is all that was built.

When you walk along the pavement, you will see lots of manhole covers. This is so that the workers who look after underground London can get to their pipes and cables. Often, roads have to be dug up so that major work can be carried out on the pipes and cables. It's always interesting to peer into a trench in the road, and see the spider's web of cables for yourself. Each manhole is covering up a different secret. One might be for telephone wires, another for water pipes. There are manholes where the people who clean the sewers can climb deep underground so that they can begin their work in the dark. And there are coal-holes. If you look carefully in some of the older parts of London, you will see highly decorated, perfectly round manhole covers on the pavement outside every house.

These were once used for coal. The coalman would pull up outside with his horse and cart, and empty bag after bag of coal into the cellars of the big houses through the coal hole.

Right up until just after the Second World War, coal was the most important fuel in London. It was used for cooking as well as heating. But since the 1950s it has been against the law to use coal in Central London, because of the pollution it causes. You might have seen photographs of London in the grip of a choking smog, which was what happened when fog mixed with coal smoke. Hundreds of people died every year from chest disease caused by the smog. The coal has gone, but the coal holes are still there, and so are the covers.

There are hundreds of different designs, all over the city, often saying who made them and when. If you tape a strong piece of paper over a coal hole and get some brass rubbing wax, you could take a copy of the different designs that you find.

Dripping tunnels

A good way to finish this lightning tour might be on a canal boat, from Little Venice up towards London Zoo. There are boat trips almost every day. As you pass Little Venice, you will come to the entrance to the Maida Hill tunnel. The boat's steerer will turn on the headlight, and the nose of the boat will enter the tunnel. Look at the moss and damp on the walls, and watch the black water move under the boat. Sometimes you might see a dead rat, floating alongside the boat. Maida Hill is only a fairly short tunnel, and you can see the other end as you enter. If you took a longer trip, you might go through the Islington Tunnel. At almost a thousand feet long, you are really in the dark. Turn up the collar on your coat, or drips of water might fall down your neck. And imagine, if you can, as you take this strange water road under London, what it must be like, deep down in the sewers, where the rats are still thriving and there is no light at the end of the tunnel.

Killing the rats

There are millions of rats living in the sewers of London. They are brown rats, which arrived from Russia in the 1700s. The plagues of London were spread by the black rat, so perhaps it is just as well that the much bigger brown rats have taken over. The brown rats are still disgusting, and they still spread disease, and so Londoners are still trying, and failing, to do something about the rat problem. In 1964, more than 650,000 rats were killed in London's sewers, but still they keep coming. In the City of Westminster, at street level, you are never more than a metre from a rat, even though you can't see it! The most common way of killing rats today is by laying poison. The poison often looks like grains of wheat, but they have been dyed blue or green, so that humans can't make the mistake of eating it. The problem is that rats only take a nibble to start with of any food they find, before coming back later to finish it off. This means that rats don't always get enough poison to kill them, and after a while, they become immune to the poison. Now there is a new breed of super rats, who are immune to all but the very newest poisons.

Scientists are always trying to come up with new poisons to kill the rats - and the rats keep coming back. In London, rats are like the rain. There is no getting away from them!

Building a new tunnel

The new high-speed link from St Pancras to the Channel Tunnel has to go under London. Otherwise, hundreds of houses would have to be knocked down to let the railway come through, and for people who live near the line, the noise and vibration from trains travelling at 180 miles per hour would be awful. The new tunnel will be much wider than the Tube tunnels. If two trains pass each other in the tunnel going so fast, they will make a huge shock wave, so the new tunnel will be 13 metres wide, to allow the trains to pass one another safely at speed. Over 20 miles of the new line will be carried under London, and to dig such a huge tunnel, new ways of building are being tried.

The best tunnellers in the world are the people of Switzerland and Austria, because their countries are so mountainous that they have to dig vast tunnels under the Alps to get their roads and railways through. The new line is being built very quickly, and has almost reached the outskirts of London. To get through the hills to the south of the city, a 2-mile-long tunnel has just been finished, and the engineers who built it used the new Austrian method, which is quite different from how Isambard and Marc Brunel built the Thames Tunnel. It was built in three sections. First the top part of the tunnel, the crown, was dug out, and the dirt (or 'spoil') was carried away to the tunnel entrance on conyeyor belts. Then it was lined with steel mesh, which is attached to the rock with 13-foot-long bolts and sprayed with special concrete, called shotcrete.

When the crown was finished, the engineers dug down to build the middle, or 'bench' section of the tunnel. The crown supports the walls while the bench is being dug and lined. Finally, the bottom section of the tunnel, called the 'invert', which is where the track will be laid, was dug away by excavators. This way of building tunnels is much faster, safer and stronger than the old way of digging a whole section at once. It is also much more accurate. Digging started at both ends of the tunnel at once. Engineers and surveyors have to do their work very carefully to make sure that both ends meet as closely as possible in the middle. The moment when the two tunnels meet, known as breakthrough, is a very anxious time for the builders. When the two ends of the North Downs tunnel met, on 8 June 2000, they were just 19 millimetres out of line. Let's hope that when the two ends of the vast new railway tunnel under London are finished, the engineers have got their sums right again!

CHAPTER EIGHT

Graves and Crypts

London has grown from the clay and the brick earth that it was built upon. In the two thousand years or more since London first became a city it has changed many times. After the Romans left, the old city inside the walls was abandoned for a time, but the Saxons started to build again. Since then, London has become one of the world's greatest cities. So far, London has survived. But one day, perhaps many thousands of years in the future, London will sink back into the earth from which it came. Nothing on Earth survives forever. But cities can live for thousands of years. People have much shorter lives. When they die, they too return to the earth. And as long as London survives, there must be graves and crypts to put the bodies in. Underground London waits for us all.

This is the city of the dead.

London is so old, and so big, that millions of people have lived and died there. There are graveyards, crypts (which were places under churches where bodies were kept) and cemeteries all over the city, far too many to visit in one quick trip. Every church and churchyard has its graves and memorials.

A good place to see a crypt (although the bodies have been removed) is St Brides, in the City of London. St Brides stood at the mouth of the River Fleet, and is a very ancient holy site. The floor has been peeled back, layer after layer, so that you can peer down into the Roman foundations. Then there are the great cemeteries, like Nunhead in South London, a strange place full of animals and flowers, or Abney Park in Stoke Newington, wild and overgrown, with crooked gravestones leaning from behind bushes.

Any cemetery is like a journey into the past; if you visit your local graveyard and read the faded words on the tombs, you'll want to find out more about the lives of the people who lie buried there. You can get records from the cemetery about who is buried where, and then you could find out even more from your local library,

by looking at old newspapers and photographs, to find out about the lives of the people in the graves. It is worth remembering that gravestones cost a lot of money, so poor people were usually buried without them in unmarked shared graves.

The poor disappeared from history at their death - if they were lucky and allowed to lie in peace. Until late in the 1800s, doctors were not supposed to keep dead bodies to practise on. The only bodies they were allowed were the corpses of people who had been hanged. It is difficult to become a doctor unless you've looked into a lot of bodies, so medical students used to buy dead bodies from grave-robbers. The robbers would creep out at night, and uncover newly buried bodies from the shared graves of the poor. Then they would sell them secretly to the medical schools. A grave-robber, or 'resurrection men' as they were also known, could earn a lot of money from selling dead bodies; £10 for a 'long' (or adult) and £5 for a 'short', as they called children.

People started guarding graveyards; so the grave robbers turned to murder to get the bodies. The two best known were Burke and Hare, who worked in Scotland. They killed at least fourteen people so that they could sell the bodies.

Grisly graves

There are some strange graves in London, and we might finish our tour of underground London by visiting some of the weirdest. Westminster Abbey contains over 3000 bodies, including kings and queens, politicians, musicians and writers.

The most moving grave is that of The Unknown Warrior, by the entrance. Here is buried the body of a soldier from the First World War. No one knows his name. This one grave is for all the thousands of lost soldiers who never had a grave of their own.

As you go around the Abbey, try and spot some of the grizzlier graves. David Livingstone, the great African explorer lies buried in the Abbey. Most of him, anyway. He died in tropical Africa, and in the heat his body could not last long before it started decomposing. So his friends took out his insides, put them in a tin box and buried them under a tree. They then pickled his body in salt, and carried it to the coast. It took them nine months before they got Livingstone's body onto a boat bound for England and the Abbey.

Most of the writer Thomas Hardy is buried in the Abbey, too, in Poet's Corner. But his heart is buried in the graveyard of the church in Dorset where he used to play music as a boy.

Or perhaps you might find the grave of John André. André was a spy for the British during the American War of Independence, in the 1780s. He was caught by the Americans with secret plans which he had stolen. The punishment for spying was death, and André was hanged and then buried near New York. But forty years later, when the British and Americans were friends, his body was dug up and sent back to London, where it was reburied in the Abbey with great honour.

Look out for the plaque to Sir Thomas Thynne, 'who was barbarously murdered' in 1682. You can see poor Sir Thomas as he dies, shot by three masked gunmen on horseback. Nearby you can see a statue of the great Admiral Sir Clowdisley Shovell. His ship was wrecked on rocks off the Scilly Isles, but Sir Clowdisley managed to swim to shore. Unfortunately, the Scilly Isles were home to the wreckers, who lured ships to their doom so that they could loot the valuable cargo. As he came ashore, a woman killed Sir Clowdisley, and stole his emerald ring. When his body was eventually found, it was sent for burial in the Abbey. Find the creepy tomb of Elizabeth Nightingale, with its statue of her husband trying to fight off Death, who takes the form of a foul skeleton.

You shouldn't miss the kings and queens, of course. The spookiest is the tomb of the Princes in the Tower, who were most probably murdered by their uncle, Richard III, in the 1480s. You can find them in the part of the Abbey known as Innocents' Corner. Their bones were bricked up in the Tower of London, and were only discovered during rebuilding work in the 1670s. King

Charles II ordered that they should be reburied in the Abbey. The king who had perhaps the silliest death was poor old George II, who died in 1760. He died sitting on the toilet, trying to have a pooh. He looks much more dignified now.

A visit to the necropolis

The Victorians were obsessed with death. No one is quite sure why. Perhaps, as health improved throughout the 1800s, death became rarer, and so more frightening. Whatever the reason, no one took death more seriously, and the huge Victorian cemeteries are well worth a visit. A large cemetery is known as a necropolis, which means, 'City of the Dead'. The best are Brompton, Kensal Green and Highgate, and you should take at least an afternoon to visit each of them. You can join the Friends of Kensal Green Cemetery, and get taken on a tour of the spooky catacombs. Brompton and Highgate have catacombs, too. Everywhere you look in the necropolis you will find famous people and beautiful and strange graves.

In Brompton, look for the ghostly children on the grave of Major Erne, for the burning airship on the grave of Sub-Lieutenant Warneford, and the lion on top of the grave of John Jackson, who was England's first heavyweight boxing champion.

In Kensal Green you can find the graves of Marc and Isambard Brunel. Don't be tempted to try riding the pony that stands on top of the Cooke family grave, or sitting in the stone armchair which marks the place where musician Henry Russell lies buried.

The West Cemetery at Highgate is the spookiest place in London. There have been stories of vampires who roam through the abandoned graveyard. You can only visit it now on a guided tour which is run by the Friends of Highgate Cemetery. The East Cemetery is still open to the public, and is much less ghastly. People come here from all over the world to visit the grave of the great philosopher Karl Marx.

Perhaps the strangest graves of all are above ground. In the entrance hall of University College sits another great philosopher, Jeremy Bentham. He didn't believe in burial, and he asked that after his death his body be embalmed and displayed. You can see him today, in his best clothes, sitting in the glass cabinet where he has been kept since his death in 1832.

And at St James Garlickhythe, in the City of London, they keep the mummified body of a man known as Jimmy Garlick, high up in the tower. No one is sure who he really was. Until a few years ago, it was possible to visit him, but naughty choirboys kept taking his body out to scare the vicar at choir practice. Now he is locked away, above the rest of the church, rather than under ground. On his coffin it says, 'As you are now, so was I. As I am now, you will be.' If you stand outside the church and look up at the tower where Jimmy is kept, you might think that sometimes it's good to look up, and see the blue sky above. Underground London can wait a little longer.

The two headless wives of Henry the Eighth

Some people say that Henry the Eighth was England's greatest king, but not if you were his wife. It is well known that Henry had six wives, and there is a little rhyme that can help you remember what happened to them. It goes

Divorced,

Beheaded,

Died.

Divorced,

Beheaded,

Survived.

The beheaded wives were Anne Boleyn and Catherine Howard, and they are both buried in the little church of St Peter ad Vincula, in the Tower of London. There are more than 1,500 bodies buried here, many of them without their heads. Huge crowds would gather to watch public executions; after the executioner had cut off their heads, he would hold it up, dripping with blood, and shout, "So end all traitors! God Save the King!"

Anne Boleyn was beheaded in 1536. Her crime was that she couldn't give Henry the son he wanted. But she did give England her greatest queen, Elizabeth I, who was the daughter of Henry and Anne. Catherine Howard was beheaded six years later, in 1542. Her crime was that she was young, and couldn't bear to give up her boyfriends, even after she was married to the King. The King was jealous, and so, whack! off came her head. The heads were reunited with the bodies, and buried together in this spooky place.

Funeral Fun

In medieval times, poor people were buried almost naked, or at best wrapped in a shroud of linen cloth. Only rich people could afford to be 'chested' , which meant to be buried in a coffin. In 1666, the year after the Great Plague of London, a law was passed that everyone should be buried in a proper woollen shroud. Coffins were only used to carry people to the burial ground, where they were taken out, so that the coffin could be used again. Richer people might be buried wearing white stockings, and there are still some older people who think that wearing white stockings is bad luck, because they should only be worn by the dead. Gypsies still prefer to be buried without a coffin. They like to be buried at a crossroads, wearing their best clothes, turned inside out.

It is still the custom to wear black clothes at a funeral, but until very recently, people would wear mourning clothes, or 'doole' for months or even years after a relative's death. In the

17th century, one Lady Fanshawe ordered in her will that her son and daughter should wear black for three years after her death, unless they got married. Queen Victoria wore nothing but black after the death of her beloved husband Albert in 1861 until her own death, forty years later.

After a death, people often hold a wake, or a funeral feast. Until a hundred years ago, it was the custom to drink wine from a cup which had been placed on the coffin.

In medieval times, and even later, people employed a 'sin-eater' to come to the funeral. The sin-eater would eat a meal which was served on the coffin. This meal meant that the sins of the dead person were passed to the sin-eater. Sin-eaters were thought of as very frightening people who were in touch with the spirits of the dead, and everyone avoided them, except at funerals when they were well paid to eat their ghastly meal. The funeral feast was known as the averil, and all the dead person's family and friends would be invited. They could be very expensive. In 1309, one menu for an averil was 'five and a half butts of cider, five pigs, one hare, five sheep, thirteen hens, noneteen geese, one and a half gallons of oysters, two hogs, nine capons, one and a half carcasses of beef and four bacons'. Poor people would only have a special kind of crispy bread, baked especially for the occassion.

In the 18th century people were often not very religious . One vicar reported finding people playing cards on the communion table during a funeral. Churchyards became neglected, and skulls and bones could often be found lying around the graves. Richer people started putting iron railings around their graves, to stop them being dug up by animals, or, worse, the grave-robbers. If you go to a cemetery today, you will often see this kind of grave.

In the old graveyards, you may notice that the graves are arranged so that the heads of the dead point to the west. This is an ancient custom, and is much older than Christianity. It is done so that people face the rising sun. To this day, some people call the east wind 'The Wind of the Dead Man's Feet'.

There are so many things to discover under your feet in London – you may already have passed over some of them without knowing it – and I hope this book will start you on a journey of discovering its fascinating secrets.

Underground Quiz

1) How old is London?

_____

2) What is the name of the Stone Age chief who gave his name to London?

_____

3) What was the Roman name for London?

_____

4) What did Audrey find under an old World War II bomb site?

_____

5) Which father and son team built the Thames Tunnel?

_____

6) Which monarch was on the throne when it was built?

_____

7) Who built London's very first drains?
a) the Irish b) the French c) the Romans d) the Saxons

_____

8) Before flush toilets, how did people dispose of the contents of their chamber pots?

_____

9) What fitting name was given to the situation in London in 1858, when the Thames was filled with sewage?

_____

10) What terrible disease was spread through unclean water in the 1800s?

_____

11) What is Joseph Bazalgette famous for?

_____

12) What is Fleet Street named after?

_____

13) What is the oldest Tube line?

_____

14) Which is the shortest journey on the whole Tube system?

_____

15) During World War II, what was in Winston Churchill's secret underground room?
a) a private toilet b) a private telephone to the American president c) a private cinema d) a train set

_____

Answers

1) Approximately 2000 years old

2) King Ludd

3) Londinium

4) The Roman Temple of Mithras

5) Marc and Isambard Kingdom Brunel

6) Queen Victoria

7) c

8) They threw them out of the window!

9) The Great Stink

10) Cholera

11) He built the main underground network of drains that we still use today

12) The Fleet River, now disappeared

13) The Metropolitan Line

14) Between Leicester Square and Covent Garden (it's much quicker to walk!)

15) b

Places to Visit

In each chapter you will find ideas on where to walk to discover the secrets beneath the city, monuments to see, rivers to trace, tunnels to walk down. However, there are some places that will need a little more planning, and we have listed these below. Happy exploring!

Museum of London, 150 London Wall, London EC2. Website: www.museum-london.org.uk

Brunel Engine House Museum, Railway Avenue, London SE16. Website: www.brunelenginehouse.org.uk

Abbey Mills Pumping Station, Abbey Lane, London E15

Thames Water Crossness Works, Belvedere Road, Abbey Wood, London SE2. By appointment. Website: www.tanton.ndi-rect.co.uk

London Transport Museum, Covent Garden Piazza, London WC2. Website: www.ltmuseum.co.uk

Imperial War Museum, Lambeth Road, London SE1. Website: www.iwm.org.uk

Chislehurst Caves, Old Hill, Chislehurst, Kent BR7. Website: www.chislehurstcaves.co.uk

Cabinet War Rooms, Clive Steps, King Charles Street, London SW1. Website: www.iwm.org.uk

Kew Bridge Steam Museum, Green Dragon Lane, Brentford, Middlesex TW8. Website: www.kbsm.org

London boat trips from Little Venice to London Zoo. London Waterbus Company. Telephone: 020 7482 2550

Kensal Green Cemetery, Harrow Road, London W10. Tours available.

Highgate Cemetery, Swains Lane, Highgate, London N6. Website: www.highgatecemetery.co.uk

St Brides, Fleet Street, London E4.

Westminster Abbey. Website: www. westminster-abbey.org

If you enjoyed this book, why not try others in the series:

RATS, BATS, FROGS AND BOGS OF LONDON
by Chris McLaren
Find out where you can find some of the amazing species
London has to offer the budding naturalist.
ISBN 1-904153-05-4

GRAVE-ROBBERS, CUT-THROATS AND POISONERS
OF LONDON
by Helen Smith
Dive into London's criminal past and meet some of its
thieves, murderers and villains.
ISBN 1-904153-00-3

DUNGEONS, GALLOWS AND SEVERED HEADS OF LONDON
by Travis Elborough
For spine-chilling tortures and blood-curdling punishments,
not to mention the most revolting dungeons and prisons you
can imagine.
ISBN 1-904153-03-8

THE BLACK DEATH AND OTHER PLAGUES OF LONDON
by Natasha Narayan
Read about some of the most vile and rampant diseases ever
known and how Londoners overcame them – or not!
ISBN 1-904153-01-1

GHOSTS, GHOULS AND PHANTOMS OF LONDON
by Travis Elborough
Meet some of the victims of London's bloodthirsty monarchs,
murderers, plagues, fires and famines - who've chosen to stick
around!
ISBN 1-904153-02-X

In case you have difficulty finding any Watling St books in your local bookshop, you can place orders directly through

BOOKPOST
Freepost
PO Box 29
Douglas
Isle of Man
IM99 1BQ

Telephone: 01624 836000
e-mail: bookshop@enterprise.net